DATE DUE

DEMCO 38-296

Scullen Middle School LMC
2815 Mistflower Lane
Naperville, IL 60564

ACE YOUR WEATHER SCIENCE PROJECT

ACE YOUR WEATHER SCIENCE PROJECT

Robert Gardner and Salvatore Tocci

GREAT SCIENCE FAIR IDEAS

Enslow Publishers, Inc.
40 Industrial Road
Box 398
Berkeley Heights, NJ 07922
USA

http://www.enslow.com

Copyright © 2010 by Robert Gardner and Salvatore Tocci

All rights reserved.

No part of this book may be reproduced by any means without the written permission of the publisher.

Library of Congress Cataloging-in-Publication Data

Gardner, Robert, 1929–
  Ace your weather science project : great science fair ideas / Robert Gardner and Salvatore Tocci.
    p. cm. — (Ace your physics science project)
  Summary: "Presents several science experiments and project ideas about weather"—Provided by publisher.
  Includes bibliographical references and index.
  ISBN-13: 978-0-7660-3223-1
  ISBN-10: 0-7660-3223-X
  1. Weather—Experiments—Juvenile literature. 2. Science projects—Juvenile literature. I. Tocci, Salvatore. II. Title.
  QC981.3.G378 2010
  551.5078—dc22

                                        2008049779

Printed in the United States of America
042011 Lake Book Manufacturing, Inc., Melrose Park, IL

10 9 8 7 6 5 4 3 2

To Our Readers:
We have done our best to make sure all Internet Addresses in this book were active and appropriate when we went to press. However, the author and the publisher have no control over and assume no liability for the material available on those Internet sites or on other Web sites they may link to. Any comments or suggestions can be sent by e-mail to comments@enslow.com or to the address on the back cover.

♲ Enslow Publishers, Inc., is committed to printing our books on recycled paper. The paper in every book contains 10% to 30% post-consumer waste (PCW). The cover board on the outside of each book contains 100% PCW. Our goal is to do our part to help young people and the environment too!

The experiments in this book are a collection of the authors' best experiments, which were previously published by Enslow Publishers, Inc., in *Science Fair Success in the Hardware Store*, *Science Project Ideas About Air*, *Science Project Ideas About Rain*, *Science Project Ideas About the Sun*, and *Science Project Ideas in the House*.

Illustration Credits: Jacob Katari, Figures 1, 5, 6–18, 19–23; National Oceanic and Atmospheric Administration/Department of Commerce, Figure 18; Stephen F. Delisle, Figures 2, 3, 4.

Photo Credits: Shutterstock

Cover Photos: Shutterstock

CONTENTS

CHAPTER 1

Air Temperature and Pressure 13

CHAPTER 2

The Science Behind the Weather 29

CHAPTER 3

Rain and the Water Cycle 45

🌀 *Indicates experiments that offer ideas for science fair projects.*

Rainbows: Light Reflection and Refraction   65

Clouds: Droplets of Water in the Sky   79

Snow: Tiny Crystals of Ice   93

🜨 *Indicates experiments that offer ideas for science fair projects.*

INTRODUCTION

When you hear the word *science*, do you think of a person in a white lab coat surrounded by beakers of bubbling liquids, specialized lab equipment, and computers? What exactly *is* science? Maybe you think science is only a subject you learn in school. Science is much more than this.

Science is the study of the things that are all around you, every day. No matter where you are or what you are doing, scientific principles are at work. You don't need special materials or equipment—or even a white lab coat—to be a scientist. Materials commonly found in your home, at school, or at a local store will allow you to become a scientist and pursue an area of interest. By making careful observations and asking questions about how things work, you can begin to design experiments to investigate a variety of questions. You can do science. You probably already have but just didn't know it!

Perhaps you are reading this book because you are looking for an idea for a science fair project for school, or maybe you are just hoping to find something fun to do on a rainy day. This book will provide an opportunity for you to learn about an area of science that affects you every day: the weather.

THE SCIENTIFIC METHOD

All scientists look at the world and try to understand how things work. They make careful observations and conduct research about a question. Different areas of science use different approaches. Depending on the phenomenon being investigated, one method is likely to be more appropriate than another. Designing a new medication for heart disease, studying the spread of an invasive plant species such as purple loosestrife, and finding evidence about whether there was once water on Mars all require different methods.

Despite the differences, however, all scientists use a similar general approach to do experiments. It is called the scientific method. In most experiments, some or all of the following steps are used: making an observation, formulating a question, making a hypothesis (an answer to the question) and prediction (an if-then statement), designing and conducting an experiment, analyzing results and drawing conclusions, and accepting or rejecting the hypothesis. Scientists then share their findings with others by writing articles that are published in journals. After—and only after—a hypothesis has repeatedly been supported by experiments can it be considered a theory.

You might be wondering how to get an experiment started. When you observe something in the world, you may become curious and think of a question. Your question can be answered by a well-designed investigation. Your question may also arise from an earlier experiment or from background reading. Once you have a question, you should make a hypothesis. Your hypothesis is a possible answer to the question (what you think will happen). Once you have a hypothesis, it is time to design an experiment.

In some cases, it is appropriate to do a controlled experiment. This means there are two groups treated exactly the same except for the single factor that you are testing. That factor is often called a variable. For example, if you want to investigate whether snow melts more under black paper than under white, two groups may be used. One group is called the control group, and the other is called the experimental group. Pieces of white and black paper of the exact same size, thickness, and weight should be used. They should be placed on top of snow so that they are exposed to sunlight of equal intensity. The two groups should be treated exactly the same. The variable is the color of the paper—it is the thing that changes, and it is the only difference between the two groups.

During the experiment, you will collect data. For example, you will measure how much snow has melted. You may also make observations about what happens to the paper or the snow. By comparing the data collected from the control group (white paper) with the data collected from the experimental group (black paper), you will draw conclusions. Since the two groups were treated exactly alike except for the color of paper, an increase in the amount of snow melted in the experimental group would allow you to conclude with confidence that increased melting is a result of the one thing that was different: paper color.

Two other terms that are often used in scientific experiments are *dependent* and *independent* variables. The dependent variable here is the melting of snow, because it depends upon paper color. The color of the paper is the independent variable because it doesn't depend on anything. The independent variable is the one the experimenter inten-tionally changes. After the data is collected, it is analyzed to see whether the hypothesis was supported or rejected. Often, the results of one experiment will lead you to a related question, or they may send you off in a different direction. Whatever the results, there is something to be learned from all scientific experiments.

SCIENCE FAIRS

Some of the experiments in this book may be appropriate for science fair projects. Experiments marked with a symbol (🏆) include a section called Science Fair Project Ideas. The ideas in this section will provide suggestions to help you develop your own original science fair project. However, judges at such fairs do not reward projects or experiments that are simply copied from a book. If you decide to use a project found in this book for a science fair, you will need to find ways to modify or extend it. This should not be difficult because you will probably find that as you do these projects, new ideas for experiments will come to mind. These new experiments could make excellent science fair projects, particularly because they spring from your own mind and are interesting to you.

Science fair judges tend to reward creative thought and imagination. However, it's difficult to be creative or imaginative unless you are really interested in your project. If you decide to do a project, be sure to choose a topic that appeals to you. Consider, too, your own ability and the cost of materials. Don't pursue a project that you can't afford.

If you decide to enter a science fair and have never done so before, you should read some of the books listed in the Further Reading section. The books that deal specifically with science fairs will provide plenty of helpful hints and lots of useful information that will enable you to avoid the pitfalls that sometimes plague first-time entrants. You will learn how to prepare appealing reports that include charts and graphs, how to set up and display your work, how to present your project, and how to relate to judges and visitors.

SAFETY FIRST

As with many activities, safety is important in science, and certain rules apply when conducting experiments. Some of the rules below may seem obvious to you, but each is important to follow.

- Have **an adult** help you whenever the book advises.

- Wear eye protection and closed-toe shoes (rather than sandals), and tie back long hair.

- Don't eat or drink while doing experiments, and never taste substances being used.

- Avoid touching chemicals.

- When doing these experiments, use only nonmercury thermometers, such as those filled with alcohol. The liquid in some thermometers is mercury. It is dangerous to breathe mercury vapor. If you have mercury thermometers, **ask an adult** to take them to a local mercury thermometer exchange location.

- Do only those experiments that are described in the book or those that have been approved by **an adult**.

- Never engage in horseplay or play practical jokes.

- Before beginning, read through the entire experimental procedure to make sure you understand all instructions. Clear extra items from your work space.

- At the end of every activity, clean all materials and put them away. Wash your hands thoroughly with soap and water.

Air Temperature and Pressure

YOU MAY NOT KNOW IT, BUT WE LIVE AT THE BOTTOM OF A VAST SEA. The sea we live in is much deeper than any ocean. We live in a sea of air called the atmosphere.

It is in the lower part of the atmosphere, within 12 km (7 mi) of Earth's surface, that we see clouds. Here raindrops and snowflakes grow and fall to the bottom of the sea of air. Winds blow, temperature and air pressure change, and tornadoes, hurricanes, and thunderstorms are produced.

At the bottom of the sea of air, at Earth's surface, our eyes sting from smog produced by automobiles and from industrial smoke. It is here that we have droughts, fog, mud, and deep snow. At the bottom of this sea we also enjoy the beauty of the air above and around us—clear blue skies, fluffy clouds, soothing breezes, frost-covered grass, colorful sunsets, and rainbows.

UP! UP! INTO THE ATMOSPHERE

Experiments using weather balloons, high-altitude airplanes, and rockets have shown that air pressure decreases as we go up into the atmosphere. You may have felt this decrease in pressure after taking off in an airplane or ascending to the top of a tall building in an elevator.

[FIGURE 1]

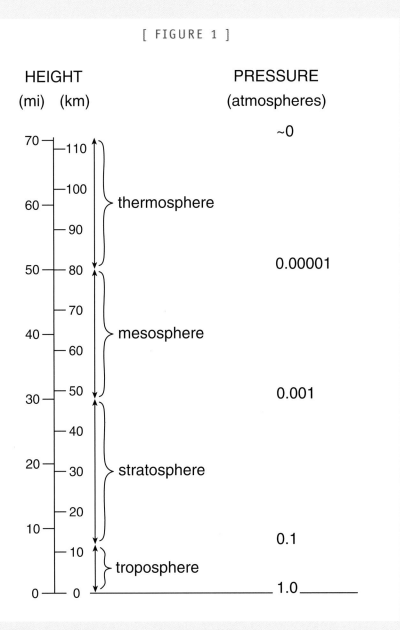

This chart shows the layers of Earth's atmosphere with their ranges of height and pressure.

These experiments have shown, too, that temperature decreases with altitude. You may have noticed that it is usually cooler on a mountaintop than in the valley below. After a certain height in the atmosphere is reached, however, the temperature begins to increase again.

Meteorologists—scientists who study weather—have divided the atmosphere into layers (see Figure 1). The first layer, the one closest to the ground, is called the troposphere. Here the temperature drops as you go up. At the top of the troposphere, about 12 km (7 mi) from the ground, the temperature is -60°C (-76°F). The height of this lowest layer of the atmosphere changes with the time of year and the distance from the equator. Near the equator, the troposphere is about 18 km (11 mi) tall. Near the North and South Poles, it is only about 6 km (4 mi) tall. The troposphere stretches higher in the summer.

Above the troposphere is the stratosphere, where the temperature rises with altitude to a maximum of about -5°C (23°F). Most of Earth's ozone is found in the stratosphere. Although there is very little of this gas in the atmosphere, it plays a very important role. It absorbs much of the ultraviolet light in sunlight. (It is the absorption of ultraviolet rays from the sun that warms the stratosphere.) The stratosphere reaches to about 50 km (30 mi) from the ground.

After the stratosphere, we enter the mesosphere. Here the temperature falls again from -5°C (23°F) to -90°C (-130°F), and the altitude increases to 80 km (50 mi). Finally, in the thermosphere, at the top of Earth's atmosphere, the temperature rises again from -90°C to -35°C (-31°F) at an altitude of about 110 km (70 mi).

Although temperatures rise and fall as we ascend into the atmosphere, air pressure continues to fall the higher into the atmosphere we go. Air pressure just about halves for every 5.5 km (3.4 mi) of altitude. Rising through the troposphere, the pressure falls from 1.0 atmosphere (atm), the pressure at sea level, to 1/10 (0.1) atm. At the top of the stratosphere, air pressure is only 1/1,000 (0.001) atm. Through the mesosphere, the pressure falls to 1/100,000 (0.00001) atm. For all practical purposes, the air pressure is zero in the thermosphere.

The "thinner" air at high altitudes makes it harder to breathe. At the tops of peaks in the Rocky Mountains, the altitude is commonly 3,700 m (12,000 ft). On these mountains, even walking makes your heart beat fast and your breathing become rapid. The low air pressure on these mountains means that you take in less oxygen with each breath. You have to breathe faster to get the oxygen you need. Your heart must beat faster to carry the reduced oxygen in your blood to the rest of your body.

With time, you can adjust to high altitude. You become acclimatized. Your body produces more red blood cells. The added cells allow more oxygen to move from your lungs to the cells of your body. You also learn to take deeper breaths so that more oxygen enters your lungs. The people who live in the Andes Mountains of South America are able to work at an altitude of 5,800 m (19,000 ft) without ill effects. At this altitude, both the air pressure and the concentration of oxygen are less than half that at sea level. Blood tests show that these people have almost twice as many red blood cells as those of people living near sea level. Their lungs are also bigger and have more surface area. This makes it possible for more of the oxygen they breathe to get into their blood.

Jet airplanes, which fly at high altitudes, have pressurized air inside the plane to prevent passengers from feeling sick or short of breath. Another way to prevent high-altitude sickness is to provide oxygen-enriched air. In *Skylab*, an American space station launched in 1973, the air the astronauts breathed had a pressure of only one third of an atmosphere. Normally, people cannot live in such air. It is the same as the air pressure at an altitude of 8,500 m (28,000 ft). But the astronauts were perfectly healthy there because the air they breathed was 70 percent oxygen at the reduced pressure. Ordinary air is only 21 percent oxygen. At the air pressure in *Skylab*, they were breathing the equivalent of air with 23 percent oxygen at normal atmospheric pressure.

Materials:
- large paper straw
- 2 pins
- tape
- cotton thread
- large, empty, cardboard box
- plastic wrap
- large elastic band
- piece of cardboard
- pen or pencil

Suppose your family has gathered for a barbecue when, suddenly, dark clouds begin to appear and cover what was once a perfectly clear, blue sky. As soon as everyone sits down to enjoy their hamburgers and hot dogs, the rain starts. While rushing to get the food inside before everything gets soaked, someone suggests that the next time a barbecue is planned, the family should check the weather report first. Someone volunteers to watch the weather channel on television.

Someone else will tune in to a weather station on the radio. Still another person will go on the Internet to check the local forecast. But you can inform your family about the chances of rain without looking at the television, listening to the radio, or checking the Internet. You can do this by using a barometer.

A barometer indicates changes in atmospheric pressure. Whenever a weather report is given, the barometric pressure is usually included. Barometric pressure is the pressure exerted by the atmosphere, or the air around you. This pressure causes a column of mercury inside a barometer to rise or fall. Barometric pressure is usually reported in the United States in a nonmetric unit—inches. The inches represent the height to which a column of mercury will rise depending on the barometric pressure. The higher the atmospheric pressure, the higher the column.

A rising barometer is an indication that the weather will be favorable because high pressure is associated with clear skies. On the other hand, a falling barometer indicates that inclement weather is approaching as a low front nears. A low-pressure area will bring with it cloudy and rainy weather. You can build your own barometer.

Do not build your barometer during a very high-pressure or low-pressure day. If you are unsure, check a local weather report that morning. Prepare a straw as shown in Figure 2. Poke a pin through one end of a straw. Tape one end of a length of cotton thread to the same end of the straw. Tape another pin to the other end of the straw. This pin will serve as a pointer.

Remove the lid from a large, empty container. A large cardboard box works well. Cover the top with plastic wrap and secure with an elastic band. Tape the free end of the cotton string to the plastic wrap. Stand a piece of cardboard securely behind the container.

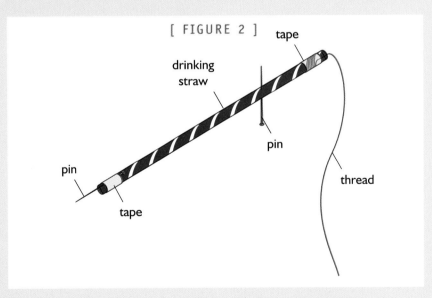

[FIGURE 2]

tape

drinking straw

pin

pin

thread

tape

The straw will function as a gauge to indicate whether the atmospheric pressure is rising or falling. The pin taped to the end of the straw will serve as a pointer that indicates a rise or fall in atmospheric pressure.

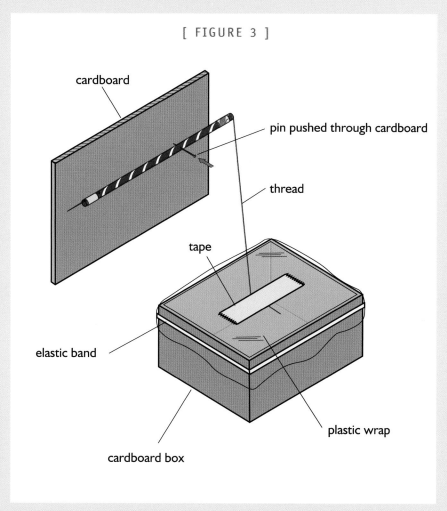

[FIGURE 3]

cardboard

pin pushed through cardboard

thread

tape

elastic band

plastic wrap

cardboard box

Once you have everything set up, make sure that no one moves the box or else your barometer will be inaccurate. Changes in barometric pressure will cause the plastic sheet covering the box to rise and fall. As it does, the thread will cause the straw to move as it pivots on the pin. As the pointer (pin) on the end of the straw moves up and down, mark the corresponding points on the cardboard. You will then have a dial to note any change in barometric pressure.

Push the pin that you pierced through the straw into the cardboard, as shown in Figure 3. Position the cardboard box so that the tension on the cotton string keeps the straw in a horizontal position.

Over the next several days, mark the cardboard to note the positions of the pin on the end of the straw. Your marks will form a dial. The top of the dial will indicate high pressure, and the bottom will indicate low pressure. You are now set to forecast the weather. As the atmospheric pressure rises, it pushes down on the plastic wrap. This increased pressure causes the straw to pivot upward. A decrease in atmospheric pressure causes the plastic wrap to move upward, allowing the straw to pivot downward. Compare your barometric changes with those of the weather forecaster on the radio, television, or Internet. Did your barometer work?

Science Fair Project Idea

An alternative to using a barometer is to use a chemical solution and filter paper to forecast the weather. Some chemicals change color, depending on whether or not they contain water. Such chemicals are known as hydrated salts. Use the library and the Internet for information on these salts. Choose one to prepare a solution that you can apply to filter paper. Apply several coats of solution, allowing the paper to dry between each application. Observe its color. Place the filter paper near an open window when it rains. Notice what happens to the color. Use what you learn to make a weather indicator to mount on the outside of your house. That way you will be able to predict the weather for your next family barbecue.

1.2 Does the Atmosphere Exert Pressure?

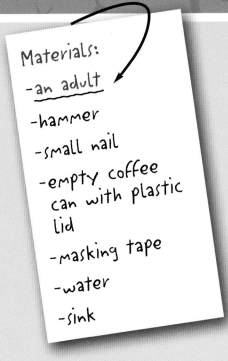

Materials:
- an adult
- hammer
- small nail
- empty coffee can with plastic lid
- masking tape
- water
- sink

In the 1600s, people used a rather simple device that depended on atmospheric pressure to forecast the weather. The device was known as a "poor man's barometer" because it was inexpensive to make. This device, called a weather glass, became a standard ship's instrument for forecasting approaching storms. You can still find weather glasses in use today in a variety of places. No matter what instrument you use, you will find that the atmosphere is always exerting pressure. See for yourself with this simple experiment.

Have an adult use a hammer and a small nail to punch three small holes on the bottom of an empty coffee can and one small hole in the plastic lid. Cover the holes in the can with masking tape. Fill the coffee can halfway with water. Place the lid on the can. Hold the can over a sink. Remove the masking tape over the holes in the can. Place your finger over the hole in the lid and press down gently. Observe what happens.

Slowly stop applying pressure on the lid. Remove your finger from the hole in the lid. Observe what happens. When you filled the can halfway with water, the remaining space was filled with air. The water inside the can was under atmospheric pressure from two sources—one above the water, the other below the water. Pushing down on the lid increased the pressure on the air above the water. As shown in Figure 4a, this pressure above the water was high enough to overcome the pressure exerted by the atmosphere on the bottom of the water. Thus the water was forced out the bottom of the can.

When you removed your finger, you stopped putting pressure on the air above the water. But the atmospheric pressure outside continued to put pressure on the bottom of the water, keeping it inside the can, as shown in Figure 4b. How might these results be different if you performed the same experiment on top of Mount Everest, where the atmospheric pressure is much lower? Experiment to see if the number of holes affects how the water is forced out of the can when you apply pressure. You can also test whether placing holes in the side of the can produces the same result. For example, try punching holes vertically down one side of a coffee can. Be sure that all the holes you make will be below the level of the water that is placed in the can.

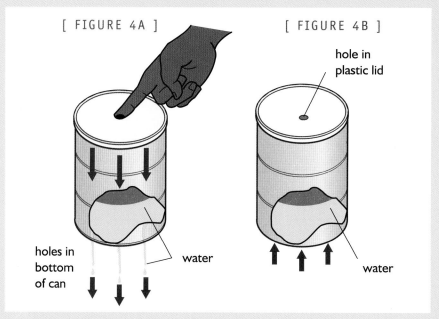

[FIGURE 4A]   [FIGURE 4B]

hole in
plastic lid

holes in
bottom
of can

water

water

a) Water pours out of the bottom of the can because of the higher pressure exerted on the water from above.
b) Because the atmospheric pressure is the same both above and below the water, the water remains in the can.

Materials:

- alcohol thermometer
- sunny day
- building such as house or school
- an outside area
- pen or pencil
- notebook
- blacktop area with grassy area nearby

You can measure temperature with a thermometer. On a bright sunny day, take a thermometer outside and measure the temperature of the air in different places. Be sure you leave the thermometer in each place for several minutes. The liquid level in the thermometer should not be changing when you read the thermometer.

Measure the outside temperature on the north side of a building such as your house or school. Then measure the temperature on the south side of the same building. Record your results. How do the temperatures compare? Can you explain any differences?

How does the air temperature over blacktop compare with the air temperature over a grassy area nearby? How does the temperature in a sunny area compare with the temperature in a shady place?

During the same day, measure the temperature on the east and west side of the building. Do this at different times of the same day. Be sure to write down your results. How do these temperatures compare? Can you explain any differences?

Science Fair Project Ideas

- If it is spring or fall, and the building is not being heated or cooled, measure some temperatures inside. How do the air temperatures in the basement, on the ground floor, and in the attic compare? Can you explain any differences in temperature that you find at these various levels?

- Measure the temperature near the floor of a room. Then measure the temperature near the ceiling. How do these two temperatures compare? Can you explain any difference in temperature that you find at these different levels in the room?

Materials:
- flashlight
- globe

Those of us who live in the Northern Hemisphere are closer to the sun in winter than we are in summer. You may have wondered how it can be colder in the winter when we are closer to the sun. To see how this is possible, shine a flashlight on a globe. Hold the flashlight so its circular beam points directly onto the Tropic of Capricorn. The Tropic of Capricorn is a line on the globe that runs around Earth 23.5 degrees south of the equator. On the first day of winter, the sun appears to follow a path that is directly over the Tropic of Capricorn. Now move the flashlight upward without changing its tilt (the direction of its beam) until its light falls on the United States. The beam should be parallel to its original direction (pointing in the same direction as before), as shown in Figure 5. (Since the sun is so far away, rays of sunlight reaching Earth are very nearly parallel.) The light now shines on a more northern part of the globe. As you can see, the flashlight beam shining on the United States no longer makes a circular pattern of light. The beam is now spread out over a much broader surface.

Because the same amount of sunlight is spread over a bigger surface, the sunlight is less intense. The same energy is spread over a much bigger area. Winter sunlight that shines directly on points south of the equator, strikes the Northern Hemisphere at a steep angle. The less intense sunlight in northern regions gives us less energy to heat that part of Earth. As a result, temperatures in the Northern Hemisphere are lower during winter months.

Continue to move the flashlight farther north along the globe without changing the direction of its beam. You will find that no light reaches the North Pole. It remains dark throughout the winter.

Now move the flashlight so that it points directly at the Tropic of Cancer. The Tropic of Cancer is a line on the globe that runs around Earth

23.5 degrees north of the equator. On the first day of summer, the sun appears to follow a path that is directly over the Tropic of Cancer.

Move the flashlight slowly northward on the globe without changing the beam's direction until its light falls on the United States. The beam should be parallel to its original direction, but slightly farther north on the globe. As you can see, the beam shining on the United States makes a nearly circular pattern of light. The same light is spread over much less area than it was when the winter sun (flashlight) was pointed at the Tropic of Capricorn. The more intense summer sunlight provides more warmth, raising temperatures in the Northern Hemisphere. What will happen in the Southern Hemisphere during our summer?

[FIGURE 5]

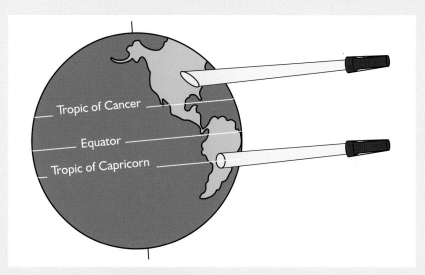

The winter sun is directly over the Tropic of Capricorn on about December 20. The sunlight striking the United States at that time is spread over a larger area and so is less intense.

Science Fair Project Idea

You have probably heard the term *global warming*. Do some research to find out more about global warming. What five years in the past century were the warmest on record? Why do you think this is so? What can be done?

The Science Behind the Weather

UNDOUBTEDLY YOU HAVE HEARD A METEOROLOGIST ON THE NEWS TALK ABOUT TEMPERATURE AND CHANCE OF RAIN OR SNOW, BUT DO YOU KNOW THE SCIENCE BEHIND TEMPERATURE AND PRECIPITATION? Do you understand the terms *humidity, dew point*, and *pressure system*?

In this chapter, you will discover how water becomes rain and fog. You will investigate why high humidity makes a warm day feel hotter, and what you can do to cool down. You will also find that even on a clear day there is water in the air all around us. If you haven't heard the forecast, you can learn how to gauge how far away a storm is.

Let's investigate the science behind the weather.

2.1 Fog and Humidity

Materials:
- jar
- ice
- hot water
- thin plastic bag
- warm water
- shiny metal can
- spoon

Find a jar with a mouth slightly smaller than the size of an ice cube. Fill the jar with hot water; then pour out all but about an inch of the water. Place an ice cube on the mouth of the jar and hold the jar up to the light. Do you see thin streams of fog forming where the warm air in the jar meets the ice?

Where did the fog come from, the ice or the warm air? Repeat the experiment, but this time wrap the ice cube in a small, thin plastic bag.

The fact that fog still forms shows that the moisture did not come from the ice. It must have come from the warm air above the hot water.

Just as sugar dissolves in water and cannot be seen, water dissolves in air. And, like particles of sugar, the particles of water are so small they cannot be seen. You may know that more sugar will dissolve in hot water than in cold water. Perhaps more water can dissolve in hot air than in cold air.

At any temperature there is a limit to the amount of sugar that will dissolve in a liter of water. When this limit is reached, we say the solution is saturated. If the temperature of a saturated sugar solution decreases, the water cannot hold as much sugar. The sugar in excess of saturation falls out of solution. Is the same true of water in the atmosphere?

To test this idea, slowly lower the temperature of some warm water in a shiny metal can. You can do this by adding small pieces of ice to the water as you stir it. If our idea is correct, water should fall out of the air (condense) when the air is cold enough to form a saturated solution of water in air. Look for signs of moisture on the outside of the can as the temperature falls. Can you find evidence to support our idea?

In the summertime you have probably seen moisture on the outside of a cold pitcher of iced tea or milk. How do you explain such moisture? Where have you seen condensed moisture in the wintertime?

Materials:

-alcohol thermometer

-ice

-warm water

-shiny metal can

-pen or pencil

-notebook

The water dissolved in air is called humidity. The amount of water dissolved in one cubic meter of air is called the absolute humidity. It can be measured using a method similar to the one you used in the previous experiment. Just repeat the second part of that experiment, but this time stir the water with a thermometer as you cool it. Record the temperature at which you first see moisture condensing on the can. This temperature is called the dew point.

Once you have found the dew point, you can use Table 1 to determine the absolute humidity. The table gives the maximum amount of

TABLE 1.

Maximum Amounts of Water Vapor in Air at Different Temperatures

Temperature (°C)	Temperature (°F)	Water vapor (g/cu m)
0	32	4.8
5	41	6.8
10	50	9.3
15	59	12.7
20	68	17.1
25	77	22.8
30	86	30.0
35	95	39.2

water that can be dissolved in one cubic meter of air at a given temperature.

You know the dew point; therefore you know the temperature at which the air in contact with the can is saturated with water vapor. For example, suppose the air in the room where you are working is 20°C (68°F), and you find the dew point to be 10°C (50°F). From the table you see that the air holds 9.3 g/m^3.

At 20°C (68°F) the air could hold 17.1 grams of moisture per cubic meter. But in our example it contains only 9.3 grams of the 17.1 grams it could hold. Therefore, it contains only 9.3/17.1, or 54 percent, of the moisture required for saturation. This ratio—the water vapor present in the air compared to the total vapor the air could hold if saturated—when expressed as a percentage, is called the relative humidity.

Use the dew point and the temperature of the air to determine the absolute and relative humidity in your kitchen. Repeat the experiment in your bathroom just after you take a shower. Which room do you think will have the greatest *absolute* humidity? The greatest *relative* humidity?

Science Fair Project Idea

Try the same experiment in various parts of your house and outdoors. Try it on clear, cloudy, and rainy days. Try it at different times of the year. What changes in absolute and relative humidity do you find?

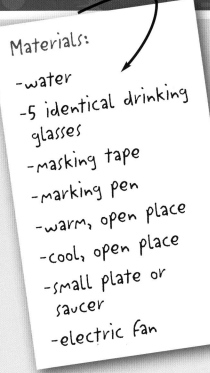

Materials:

- water
- 5 identical drinking glasses
- masking tape
- marking pen
- warm, open place
- cool, open place
- small plate or saucer
- electric fan

Most of the moisture in air comes from lakes and oceans through a process called evaporation. To see what evaporation is, fill five identical drinking glasses about three-fourths full of water. Line the glasses up and be sure they all contain the same volume. Using masking tape and a marking pen, make a mark on each glass at the water level.

Put one glass in a warm, open place (on a radiator might be a good location). Put another in a cool, but not freezing, open place (near a window in the wintertime would be good). Leave the third one at room temperature. Place the fourth near the third, but cover it with a small plate or saucer. The fifth glass should be placed in front of an electric fan.

Mark the water levels in each glass over a period of several days. Which glass seemed to lose the most water? Which one lost none? What effect did temperature have on the water lost?

The escape of water from its surface is called evaporation. Where do you think the water goes? What was the purpose of the covered glass in this experiment?

Science Fair Project Idea

What factors might increase or decrease evaporation? Design and conduct an experiment to test the effect of some of these factors on evaporation.

2.4 How Does Evaporation Cause Cooling?

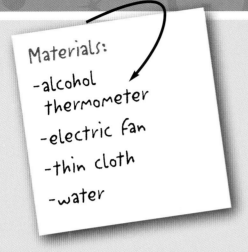

Materials:
- alcohol thermometer
- electric fan
- thin cloth
- water

On a hot summer day, what can you do to cool off if you do not have an air conditioner?

If you are outside, you might look for a place where there is a breeze. If you are indoors, you might turn on a fan. In a moving car you could open a window and let the air flow over you. All these ways of getting cool involve moving air. Is moving air really cooler than still air?

To find out, place a thermometer in a room. After a few minutes record the temperature. Now place a fan in front of the thermometer. Does the temperature go up, down, or remain the same? Is moving air cooler than still air?

Swimming is another way to get cool on a hot day. In fact, when you get out of the water and stand in a breeze, you may feel cold and start to shiver. You know the moving air is not cold; cooling off must have something to do with your wet skin. Could the evaporation of water from your skin make you feel cold?

You know from the previous experiment that water evaporates faster when air is moving over it. To see if rapid evaporation can cool a moist object, soak a strip of thin cloth in water. Wrap the cloth around the bulb of an alcohol thermometer. When the liquid in the thermometer tube stops moving, note the temperature. Then hold the thermometer in front of a fan or swing it through the air for a few minutes. What happens to the temperature?

Evaporation happens because the fastest-moving molecules in a liquid are constantly leaving the surface to become a gas. When water evaporates, it becomes the gas—the water vapor—that makes up the humidity in the air. Because the fastest-moving molecules are the warmest ones, the ones that remain behind in the liquid are the cooler ones; hence the liquid becomes cooler as it evaporates.

2.5 How Does the Rate of Evaporation Affect Cooling?

Materials:
- hot water
- 3 identical aluminum pie pans
- newspaper
- 3 alcohol thermometers
- cooking oil
- electric fan
- watch or clock
- pen or pencil
- notebook

Knowing that a liquid cools as it evaporates, try to predict how the *rate* of evaporation will affect the temperature of an evaporating liquid.

To check your prediction, pour equal amounts of hot water into three identical aluminum pie pans. Place the pans on folded newspapers for insulation. Submerge a thermometer in each pan. To keep the evaporation rate near zero in one pan, add a few drops of cooking oil to cover the water. Leave a second pan undisturbed. To increase the rate of evaporation in the third pan, use an electric fan to blow air across it, but make sure the air from the fan does not go near the other two pans.

Record the temperature in each pan at one-minute intervals for a few minutes. In which pan does the water cool fastest? Did you predict correctly?

Can you explain why sweating keeps you cool?

2.6 Can You Make Rain?

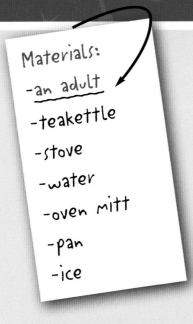

Materials:
- an adult
- teakettle
- stove
- water
- oven mitt
- pan
- ice

You have seen that warm air holds more moisture than cold air. You have seen also that when the temperature falls below the dew point, water vapor in the air begins to fall out of solution.

Using these principles, you can make it rain in your kitchen. **Under adult supervision**, heat a teakettle of water to boiling on the kitchen stove. **(Be careful using the stove. Be sure to turn it off when you are finished.)** Using an oven mitt, hold a pan of ice in the stream of steam emerging from the teakettle. Can you make it "rain" from the bottom of the cold pan?

2.1 Can You Make a Cloud?

Materials:

- an adult
- cold water
- clear glass bottle with one-hole rubber stopper
- wooden matches
- air pump
- safety glasses
- alcohol thermometer

The formation of rain droplets in the atmosphere is more complex than the "kitchen rain" you produced in the previous experiment. Tiny droplets of rain form on minute particles of salt or dust that are known as condensation nuclei. And the water vapor is cooled by its expansion as it ascends into the upper atmosphere, where there is less pressure.

You can see this effect for yourself. Put some cold water in a clear glass bottle. **Be sure the bottle has no cracks.** Shake the bottle with your hand over its mouth to saturate the enclosed air with water vapor. **Have an adult** light a match, then blow it out and let the smoke escape into the mouth of the inverted bottle. The smoke particles will serve as condensation nuclei so that droplets of water can form as the water vapor cools. To cool the air and vapor, connect an air pump to a one-hole rubber stopper and put the stopper into the bottle's mouth. **Put on safety glasses now.** Pump air into the bottle until you pop the stopper. The expansion of the pressurized air will cool the vapor, causing it to condense into tiny droplets that form a cloud inside the bottle.

Just as expansion causes a gas to cool, so compression will cause a gas to become warmer. To see this effect, use an air pump to force compressed air across the bulb of a thermometer. What happens to the temperature?

In a diesel engine the compression of the fuel vapor produces a temperature high enough to ignite the vapor. As a result, diesel engines, unlike gasoline engines, do not have spark plugs.

2.8 Air Pressure

Materials:

- an adult
- pail or sink
- water
- drinking glass
- index card
- one-gallon metal can with cap or rubber stopper to fit opening
- stove
- pot holders or oven mitts
- cardboard sheet or heatproof mat

To see that air really does exert a pressure, try these experiments.

Fill a pail or sink with water. Submerge a drinking glass and fill it. Turn the glass under water so that it is upside down, and slowly lift it until most of it, but not the open end, is out of the water. As you can see, the water in the glass is well above the water level in the sink. Normally, gravity would cause water to fall from the glass. What is keeping the water up?

Fill a glass to the brim with water. Place an index card on the glass. Put your hand on top of the card and invert the glass of water over the sink. Remove your hand. Why doesn't the card fall from the glass and the water spill out?

Here is an even more dramatic experiment to show the presence of air pressure. In this experiment you will get rid of the air that is normally inside a container. Then you will be able to see the effect of the force that air pressure exerts when there is little or no opposing force. **Ask an adult** to help you with this experiment.

Take a one-gallon metal can like the ones that paint thinner and olive oil come in. If the can's screw-on cap is missing, use a rubber stopper that fits the opening in the can.

Rinse the can thoroughly to remove any flammable liquid that might remain. Pour a cup of water into the can. Leave the top of the can open and heat the can on the stove. Steam from the boiling water will drive air out of the can. Let the water boil for several minutes to be sure that most of the air is gone.

Using oven mitts or pot holders to protect your hands, remove the can from the heat and place it on a thick piece of cardboard or a heat-proof mat. Immediately seal the can with its screw-on cap or a rubber stopper.

As the can cools, the steam will condense, leaving the can very nearly empty. Watch how the air outside the can, unopposed now by air that is normally inside, pushes inward on all sides of the can. Were you amazed by the strength of air?

2.9 How Far Away Is the Storm?

Materials:

-stopwatch, or clock or watch with second hand
-stormy weather

You may know that thunder is caused by the expansion of air heated by a lightning stroke. But the speed of sound (331 meters per second or 1/5 mile per second) is negligible compared with the speed of light (300,000 kilometers per second or 186,000 miles per second). That is why you see lightning before you hear thunder.

Because the light from lightning reaches your eyes almost instantaneously, you can use the time delay between the sight of lightning and the sound of the thunder it creates to determine how far away the lightning is. Count the number of seconds between the lightning and the thunder. Since sound travels 1/3 kilometer per second or 1/5 mile per second, it takes 3 seconds to go one kilometer and 5 seconds to go one mile. If you divide the number of seconds between lightning and thunder by 5, you will have the distance to the lightning in miles. How would you find the distance in kilometers?

Repeat the experiment every few minutes. Is the storm approaching or moving away?

Rain
and the
Water Cycle

WITHOUT WATER WE CANNOT LIVE, AND THAT WATER COMES TO US FIRST AS RAIN. Rain seeps into soil and nurtures the plants that we and other animals eat. It fills our wells, lakes, and ponds. Rain that drains away into rivers provides a highway for ships, water for irrigation, and energy to make electric power.

Water, the basis of life, is also the lifeblood of agriculture and industry. Every bushel of corn requires about 13,000 liters (3,400 gallons) of water. A similar amount of rain is needed to produce a pound of beef. It takes about 450 liters (120 gallons) to produce each egg you eat. To process one ton of wood pulp, 225,000 liters (60,000 gallons) of water are used; distilling 15 liters (4 gallons) of gasoline requires more than 150 liters (40 gallons) of water; and 150,000 liters (40,000 gallons) of water are needed to manufacture one automobile. An average American uses more than 450 liters of water every day.

Each day more than a quadrillion liters of rain fall on Earth. (A quadrillion is a one followed by 15 zeros.) In a single year, 491 quadrillion liters (130 quadrillion gallons) of rain fall on Earth. A little more than one fifth of that rain falls on land. Spread evenly over Earth, the total rainfall (if it didn't evaporate) would cover Earth with a layer of water almost one meter (38 inches) deep. But rain does not fall evenly over Earth's surface. In some places, a lot of rain falls; in other places it seldom rains. For example, on Mount Waialeale in Hawaii, 11.7 meters (460 inches) of rain fall each year. At Kharga Oasis in Egypt, only a trace of rain is detected.

Materials:

- large container such as a coffee can or peanut butter jar
- narrow transparent container such as an olive jar or graduated cylinder
- ruler
- water
- masking tape
- marking pen
- stake
- nail
- hammer
- open area
- string or wire
- rain

Rain is usually measured in millimeters (mm) or inches (in). You can make a simple rain gauge that will allow you to measure how much rain falls during a storm. Any large container with straight sides can be used to collect rain. A coffee can or a large peanut butter jar works well. Why should you NOT use a jar with a mouth that is narrower than the rest of the jar?

Rainfalls often produce less than 25 mm (1 in) of rain. Small amounts of rain are difficult to measure accurately in a large container. You can measure more accurately by pouring any water you collect into a narrower transparent container with straight sides, such as the kind of jar that olives come in. To put measurements on the narrow jar, pour water into the large container until the water is exactly 25 mm (1.0 in) deep. Then pour that water into the narrow jar. Place a strip of masking tape along the side of the narrow jar. Mark the height of the water on the tape and label it 25 mm (1.0 in). Divide the distance from the mark to the bottom of the jar into ten equal spaces (see Figure 6a). Each line corresponds to 2.5 mm (0.1 in) of rain. If the jar holds more than 25 mm of water, you can continue to mark the tape to the top of the jar with equally-spaced lines. How can you measure more than 25 mm of rain if the smaller jar will hold no more than 25 mm of rain?

Before the next rain falls, use string or wire, and a nail, to tie the large, empty container to the top of a stake in an open area far from trees, bushes, and buildings, as shown in Figure 6b. Why should you measure the rain you've collected as soon as possible after the rain stops?

If you are very ambitious, measure and record rainfall over the course of a year or more. Is there one time of the year when more rain falls? Is there a period during which little rain falls? What is the total precipitation (rainfall and melted snowfall) for an entire year? (See Experiment 6.1 to find out how to convert inches of snowfall to depth of rain.)

Table 2 shows the annual precipitation (rainfall and melted snowfall) at a number of United States weather stations. How does your measure-ment of annual precipitation compare with that given for the weather station in Table 2 that is nearest you?

THE WATER CYCLE

Rain is only one part of the water cycle, a cycle that keeps Earth's water circulating. A third of the rain that falls on land runs off into rivers. The rivers carry water back to the ocean from which most of it came. The water in lakes, ponds, rivers, and oceans (which contain more than 95 percent of Earth's water) is constantly evaporating. During evaporation, water changes from a liquid to a gas. The gaseous water becomes mixed with the other components of air— mostly nitrogen and oxygen.

Evaporation occurs throughout the world. But evaporation is greatest from warm ocean water near the equator. The moist air over the equator rises and is carried northward and southward by winds. As the moist air

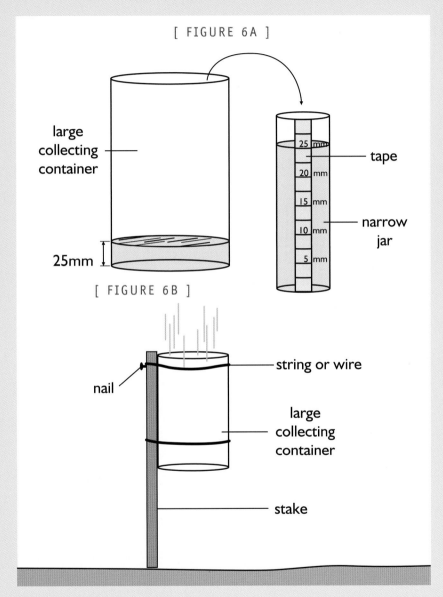

[FIGURE 6A]

large collecting container

25mm

25 mm — tape

20 mm

15 mm

10 mm — narrow jar

5 mm

[FIGURE 6B]

string or wire

nail

large collecting container

stake

a) A large container with 25 mm (1.0 in) of water. The water is poured into a narrow container so that rainfall can be measured more accurately. b) Before a rain, tie the large collecting container to a vertical stake in an open area.

TABLE 2.

Normal annual precipitation for a number of U.S. cities to nearest millimeter (or inch).

Station Location	Precipitation in mm (in)
Mobile, Alabama	1,626 (64)
Anchorage, Alaska	406 (16)
Phoenix, Arizona	203 (8)
Little Rock, Arkansas	1,829 (72)
Los Angeles, California	381 (15)
San Francisco, California	508 (20)
Denver, Colorado	381 (15)
Hartford, Connecticut	1,118 (44)
Wilmington, Delaware	1,041 (41)
Washington, D.C.	991 (39)
Jacksonville, Florida	1,295 (51)
Miami, Florida	1,422 (56)
Atlanta, Georgia	1,295 (51)
Honolulu, Hawaii	559 (22)
Boise, Idaho	305 (12)
Chicago, Illinois	914 (36)
Indianapolis, Indiana	1,016 (40)
Des Moines, Iowa	838 (33)
Lexington, Kentucky	1,143 (45)
New Orleans, Louisiana	1,575 (62)
Portland, Maine	1,041 (41)
Baltimore, Maryland	1,067 (42)

Station Location	Precipitation in mm (in)
Boston, Massachusetts	1,067 (42)
Detroit, Michigan	838 (33)
Duluth, Minnesota	762 (30)
Jackson, Mississippi	1,397 (55)
Kansas City, Missouri	965 (38)
Helena, Montana	305 (12)
Omaha, Nebraska	762 (30)
Reno, Nevada	203 (8)
Atlantic City, New Jersey	1,016 (40)
Albany, New York	914 (36)
Raleigh, North Carolina	1,041 (41)
Bismark, North Dakota	381 (15)
Cleveland, Ohio	940 (37)
Portland, Oregon	914 (36)
Philadelphia, Pennsylvania	1,041 (41)
Providence, Rhode Island	1,168 (46)
Charleston, South Carolina	1,321 (52)
Rapid City, South Dakota	432 (17)
Memphis, Tennessee	1,321 (52)
Houston, Texas	1,168 (46)
Burlington, Vermont	864 (34)
Richmond, Virginia	1,092 (43)
Seattle-Tacoma, Washington	940 (37)
Milwaukee, Wisconsin	838 (33)
Lander, Wyoming	330 (13)

Source: U.S. Census Bureau

cools, gaseous water changes back to a liquid. The change from gas to liquid is called condensation. We say the gas condenses to a liquid. At first, the condensed droplets are tiny. They remain suspended in the air as clouds. Under certain conditions, the droplets join together to form larger drops that fall to Earth as rain. This completes the water cycle (see Figure 7).

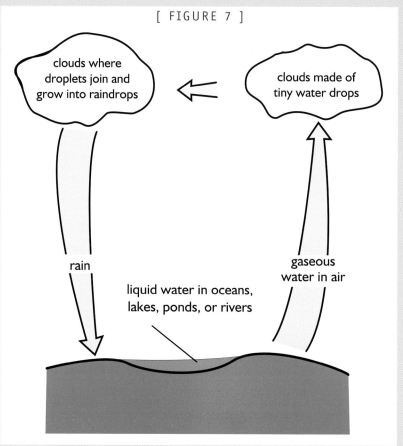

[FIGURE 7]

clouds where droplets join and grow into raindrops

clouds made of tiny water drops

rain

gaseous water in air

liquid water in oceans, lakes, ponds, or rivers

The water cycle: Water evaporates into the atmosphere as a gas. When the gaseous water cools, it condenses into tiny droplets. These droplets join to form larger drops that fall to Earth as rain.

3.2 Evaporating Water

Materials:

- -2 saucers
- -warm area
- -drinking glass
- -water
- -file cards
- -pen or pencil
- -salt
- -measuring teaspoon
- -magnifying glass

Place a saucer in a warm place in your house. Fill a drinking glass about halfway with water. Pour a small amount of the water onto the saucer. On a card write "plain water." Place the card beside the saucer.

Add 2 tsp of salt to the water that remains in the glass. Stir until the salt dissolves. Place another saucer near the first one. Pour the same amount of the salty water onto the second saucer. On another card write "salt water." Place this card beside the second saucer.

Watch these two saucers over the next few hours and into the next day or two. What happens to the amount of water that remains in the saucers? How can you explain what happens? Could you tell which saucer contained the salty water even if the cards beside the saucers were lost?

Use a magnifying glass to look closely at the salt crystals on the saucer that held the salt water. What is the shape of these crystals?

3.3 A Model of the Water Cycle

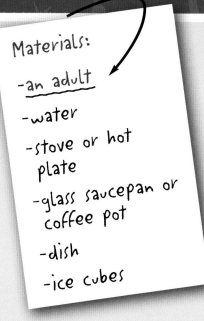

Materials:

- an adult
- water
- stove or hot plate
- glass saucepan or coffee pot
- dish
- ice cubes

The water that evaporated in Experiment 3.2 became mixed with the air in the room. It added moisture to the air, but it probably did not condense and fall as rain. To see a model of the complete water cycle, **ask an adult** to help you heat some water in a glass saucepan or coffee pot on a stove or hot plate. Place a dish with some ice cubes in it over the top of the saucepan or coffee pot, as shown in Figure 8. Heat the water until it is hot but not boiling. You will see water that has evaporated begin to condense on the bottom of the cold dish. What happens as the drops of condensed water grow larger by joining with one another?

In this model of the water cycle, what corresponds to the ocean? What represents a cloud? Where is the rain in this model?

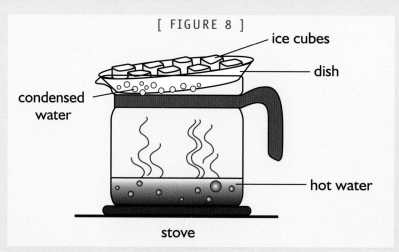

[FIGURE 8]

ice cubes

dish

condensed water

hot water

stove

A model of the water cycle can be made quite easily.

Materials:

- baking pan and cover
- baking flour
- ruler
- rain
- open area
- tweezers
- paper
- magnifying glass
- pen or pencil
- notebook
- waxed paper
- tape
- cardboard
- coffee can
- nylon stocking
- rubber band
- powdered sugar

How big is a raindrop? That was a question asked more than a century ago by W.A. Bentley, a farmer from Jericho, Vermont. You can do experiments similar to his and find the size of raindrops for yourself.

Fill a baking pan with at least 2.5 cm (1 in) of flour. Cover the pan and carry it out into an open area where rain is falling. **Do not go outside during a thunderstorm!** Remove the cover for a few seconds so that raindrops can fall into the flour. The rain will form tiny pellets when they collide with the flour. Cover the pan again and take it inside.

Allow at least an hour for the pellets to dry. Then use tweezers to remove a few dry pellets from the pan. Place the pellets on a clean piece of paper. With a ruler and a magnifier estimate the width of each pellet (probably in mm), as shown in Figure 9. Record your results. Were the raindrops all the same size? If not, what were the smallest and largest drops that fell into the flour?

You can determine the volume of the drops (pellets) as well. The volume of a drop is approximately equal to half the width cubed. That is:

Volume = 1/2 (width)^3 or

Volume = 1/2 (width x width x width)

For example, if the width of a pellet is 2 mm, its volume is approximately:

Volume = 1/2 x (2 mm)^3 =

1/2 x (2 mm x 2 mm x 2 mm) =

1/2 x 8 cubic millimeters (cu mm) = 4 cu mm

What was the volume of the largest raindrop you collected? What was the volume of your smallest raindrop?

[FIGURE 9]

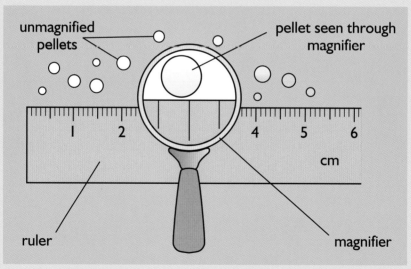

You can measure the diameter of a raindrop. The ruler shown is a centimeter (cm) ruler. Each centimeter is divided into 10 millimeters (mm). One inch = 2.54 cm, so a millimeter is about 0.04 (4/100) inch.

In a gentle rain where very fine drops are drifting to the ground, collect some droplets on a piece of waxed paper taped to a sheet of cardboard (Figure 10). Be sure the drops do not spatter when they land! These drops will form hemispheres (a ball cut in half) on the waxed paper.

Take the drops to a covered place, preferably one that is outside where the drops will not evaporate very fast. Measure their widths with a ruler and magnifier. Record your results. What is the largest drop you can find? What is the smallest drop you can find?

Here, because you are measuring hemispheres (half of a sphere), the volume is approximately one quarter of the width cubed. That is:

Volume = $1/4$ (width)^3 or

Volume = $1/4$ (width x width x width)

For example, if the width of a hemisphere is 2 mm, its volume is approximately:

Volume = $1/4$ (2 mm)^3 =

$1/4$ x 8 cu mm = 2 cu mm

[FIGURE 10]

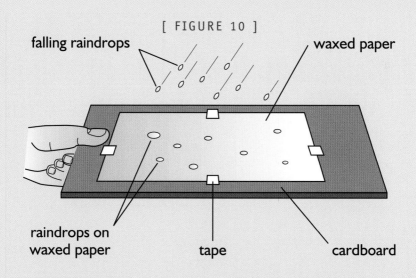

falling raindrops   waxed paper

raindrops on
waxed paper   tape   cardboard

Very small raindrops can be collected on waxed paper.

Here is still another method for measuring the size of raindrops. It was unknown to Bentley because nylon had not been invented when he did his work. Cover the open top of an empty coffee can with a piece of nylon stocking. Hold the nylon in place with a rubber band stretched around the can near its top. Sprinkle a thin layer of powdered sugar on the nylon. Cover the sugar-coated nylon with a sheet of cardboard and take it outside into the rain. Remove the cardboard cover for a couple of seconds so that a few raindrops can fall through the sugar and into the can. The drops will dissolve the sugar, leaving measurable circles as they pass through the nylon. Use a ruler and magnifier to measure the diameter of the circles. (A circle's diameter is the width or distance across the circle.) How large were the raindrops? What were their volumes?

Science Fair Project Ideas

As your skill in collecting and measuring rain-drops improves, carry out experiments to answer these and other questions:

- Does the average size of the raindrops change as a storm progresses?
- Are the raindrops that fall in a summer rain larger than those that fall in the winter?
- Are the raindrops that fall during a brief shower larger than those that fall in a long, steady rain?
- How many average-size raindrops are in a snowflake? In a hailstone?

3.5 The Shape of Raindrops

Materials:

- vacuum cleaner that will blow air
- food coloring
- water
- small glass
- eyedropper
- Ping-Pong ball

When raindrops fall in still air, they fall at a steady speed. This steady speed is called the terminal velocity of the raindrops. As you might guess, big drops have a higher terminal velocity than small drops. But all drops have a terminal velocity. In a wind tunnel, air can be directed upward until it keeps raindrops in place. The air will move by the drop at the same speed that the drop would fall through the air at its terminal velocity. You have experienced something similar when you ride a bike. Riding your bike at 19 kph (12 mph) through still air provides the same movement of air against your face as does a 19-kph (12-mph) wind when you stand still.

Artists often draw tear-shaped raindrops, but what is the actual shape of a raindrop? If you have a vacuum cleaner that will blow air, as well as draw air into the machine, you can investigate the shape of raindrops. The air stream from the vacuum cleaner will take the place of a much more expensive wind tunnel.

Add a drop or two of food coloring to some water in a small glass. Use an eyedropper to place a drop of the colored water in an upward-directed stream of air from the vacuum cleaner. To help you locate the stream, place a Ping-Pong ball in the air stream. The ball will remain in the center of the flowing air. You will have to experiment until you find a place where the drops fall very slowly. The drops you see look just like raindrops falling at a steady speed through air. What is the shape of falling raindrops?

3.6 Splashing of Raindrops

Materials:
- eyedropper
- glassful of water
- food coloring
- ruler
- camera (optional)
- fast black-and-white film (optional)
- a friend (optional)
- white paper
- different surfaces (wood, aluminum foil, various soils, concrete, etc.)
- waxed paper
- tape
- cardboard
- books or blocks

You have probably watched raindrops falling into a pond or puddle. Each raindrop makes a ring of small waves that travel outward in circles. The centers of these circles mark the place where the drop struck the water. Watch a drop closely as it falls into water. You may be able to see a jet of water rise up above the point where the drop lands.

To see such a jet, use an eyedropper to release a drop into a glassful of water. Adding food coloring to the water will help you see the drop. Hold a ruler next to the glass. How far do the drops have to fall before they produce jets? It takes place so fast that you won't be able to see all that happens, but you can see the jets and the tiny drop that breaks off from the top of the jet. If you have a good camera, you may be able to take pictures of what happens. With fast black-and-white film and good lighting, have a friend release the drops while you take pictures. It will take a large number of photos to capture the progress of the event, but you will enjoy seeing what happens if you are successful. It is a good idea to practice with an empty camera before you actually start taking photographs. After a few trials, you will be able to judge the time it takes for the drop to reach the water after it is released.

You can also see what happens to raindrops that fall on dry surfaces. Tape a sheet of white paper to a flat surface. Let drops of colored water fall from an eyedropper onto the paper. Hold the eyedropper at different heights above the paper—1 cm, 5 cm, 15 cm, 30 cm, 60 cm, 90 cm, and higher (0.5 in, 2 in, 6 in, 1 ft, 2 ft, 3 ft, and higher). How does the splash pattern made when the drop lands change as the height increases? Do you reach a height after which the pattern does not change?

Does the kind of surface the drop lands on affect the splash pattern? To find out, you can let the drops fall on wood, aluminum foil, various soils, concrete, and other kinds of material. Try letting the drops fall on waxed paper. Because waxed paper repels water, you might expect the splash pattern to be different. Try to predict what the pattern will be like. Then check your prediction. Is the pattern what you expected it would be?

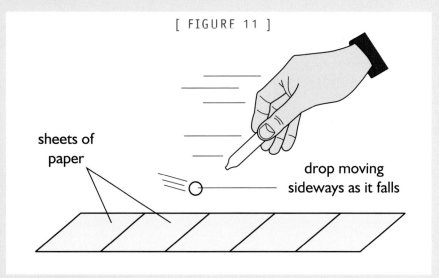

[FIGURE 11]

sheets of paper

drop moving sideways as it falls

What does the splash pattern look like if a drop is moving sideways when it lands?

Place several sheets of paper end to end on a flat surface (Figure 11). Then see what happens to the splash pattern if the drop is moving sideways when you release it. This is the way raindrops land if they are driven by a wind as they fall. How does the pattern change if you increase the speed at which the eyedropper is moving when you release the drop?

Suppose the drops fall on a "hill" (Figure 12) instead of a flat surface. Do you think this will affect the splash pattern? To find out, tape some paper to a sheet of cardboard. Rest one end of the cardboard on some books or blocks so that the paper is inclined (tilted) instead of flat. Is the splash pattern different on a hill than on a flat surface? Try to predict what will happen to the splash pattern if you make the hill steeper. Try to predict what will happen if you make it less steep. Test your predictions. Are the patterns what you expected them to be?

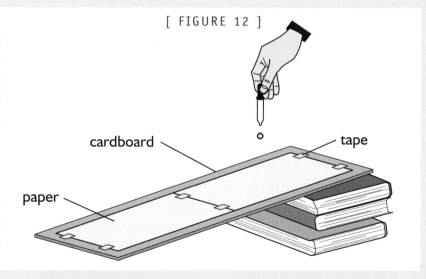

[FIGURE 12]

cardboard

tape

paper

How does an incline affect a raindrop's splash pattern?

3.7 Acid Rain

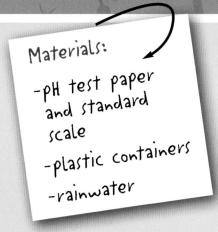

Materials:

-pH test paper and standard scale

-plastic containers

-rainwater

Many of the gases that pollute the atmosphere dissolve in cloud droplets and fall to Earth as acid rain. The strength of acids is measured in terms of pH. Neutral substances, such as pure water, have a pH of 7.0. Substances with a pH less than 7.0 are said to be acidic. Substances with a pH greater than 7.0 are alkaline.

Many people don't realize that almost all rain is slightly acidic. In fact, it is quite normal to find rain with a pH as low as 5.6. That is why acid rain is defined as rainwater that has a pH less than 5.6. Acid rain can cause the pH of water in ponds, lakes, and streams to fall to a level that kills the eggs and seeds of various animals and plants.

To find the pH of rainwater, you can collect rain in plastic containers and test it with pH paper. By comparing the color of the pH test paper dipped in rainwater with a standard found on the container that holds the test paper, you can determine the pH of the rainwater.

You will need to use test paper that can measure pH to at least ± 0.5. That is, the paper should be able to distinguish pH 4.5 from pH 4.0 or pH 5.0. If your school does not have such test paper, you can buy it from a science supply house or from a store that sells fish or swimming pool supplies.

Test rainwater for pH at different times during a storm. Does the pH change as the storm progresses?

Test rainwater for pH at different times of the year. Does the pH of rain change from season to season? Is pH related to where you live? That is, is the rain in some parts of the country or world more acidic than in other places? A reference source will help you to find out. Would you guess that snow is acidic? How can you find out?

Chapter 4

Rainbows: Light Reflection and Refraction

ONE OF THE MOST BEAUTIFUL SIGHTS ASSOCIATED WITH RAIN IS THE APPEARANCE OF A RAINBOW. Of course, not every rainy day has a rainbow. For a rainbow to appear, there must be both rain and sunlight. Furthermore, the sun must be fairly low in the sky. To see a rainbow, stand with your back to the sun and look approximately 40 degrees above the horizon (about halfway between the horizon and the area of sky directly above your head). You will see the sunlight reflected to your eyes from the falling raindrops. If the sun is very bright, you may be able to see a second, fainter rainbow about 10 degrees above the first one. If you look closely, you can see that the order of the colors in the second rainbow (violet [top], blue, green, yellow, orange, red [bottom]) is the reverse of those in the brighter one.

4.1 How Does a Rainbow Form?

Materials:
- garden hose
- a friend
- sunlight

On a sunny day, you can make a rainbow in your yard. Turn a garden hose nozzle until it produces a fine spray. Have a friend hold the nozzle so that it sprays the water up into the air while you look at the falling drops with your back to the sun. You should be able to see a beautiful rainbow in the sunlight reflected from the tiny water drops to your eyes. Which color is at the top of this rainbow? Which color is at the bottom? Can you see a second, fainter rainbow above the first one? If you can see a second rainbow, which color is at the top of this rainbow? Which color is at the bottom? After you have watched the rainbow for a while, let your friend enjoy the colors while you hold the hose.

4.2 Light Reflected in a Raindrop

Materials:

-eyedropper
-water
-paper clip
-lightbulb
-meterstick or yardstick
-round-bottom (Florence) flask or brandy glass

If you have ever looked at the surface of a quiet pond, you know that light can be reflected by water. To see the light reflected from a drop of water, use an eyedropper to place a drop of water on a bent paper clip, as shown in Figure 13a. Hold the drop about a meter (a yard) to one side of a lightbulb (Figure 13b). Look for images of the bulb reflected from both the front and rear surfaces of the drop. If you have trouble seeing these small images, try using a much larger "drop." You can make such a drop by filling a round-bottom flask (Florence flask) or a brandy glass with water. Hold this large drop about a meter (a yard) to one side of a lightbulb. Can you see images of the bulb reflected from the front and rear surfaces of the big drop? What do you notice about the images reflected from the rear surface of the drop?

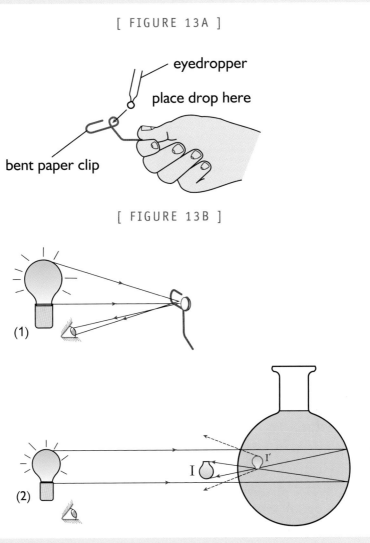

[FIGURE 13A]

eyedropper

place drop here

bent paper clip

[FIGURE 13B]

(1)

(2)

I

I′

a) A water-drop mirror with curved reflecting surfaces can be made by placing a drop of water on a bent paper clip. b) Look for light reflected from the drop (1), or from a larger "drop" in a round flask or brandy glass (2). You should be able to see an upside-down image, I, reflected from the rear surface of the drop and an upright image, I′, reflected from the front surface.

Materials:

- lightbulb
- magnifying glass
- white file card
- eyedropper
- water
- paper clip
- magazine with fine print
- round-bottom (Florence) flask or brandy glass

You have seen that light is bent (refracted) when it enters water or glass at an angle. The change in the light's path cannot be the same for all colors. You know this is true because of the experiments you have done. You have seen that it is only after the path of a light beam is bent by water or glass that the colors in the light appear. Violet light is separated from the other colors in white light because it is bent more than other colors in the light. Red light is separated because it is bent less than the other colors in white light. The difference in the amount that different colors in white light are bent accounts for the various rainbows you have seen, including nature's own true rainbow.

In a natural rainbow, light must be both refracted and reflected by the raindrops. You can show that a raindrop can bend light just as a glass or plastic lens can. First, place a single lightbulb on one side of an otherwise dark or dimly lighted room. Stand on the other side of the room and hold a magnifying glass (lens) in front of a white file card. Move the lens back and forth, closer to and farther from the card until you see a clear image of the lightbulb on the card. Is the image of the lightbulb right side up or upside down?

Figure 14a shows how the lens must have bent the light in order to form the image you saw on the white card. You can also use the same

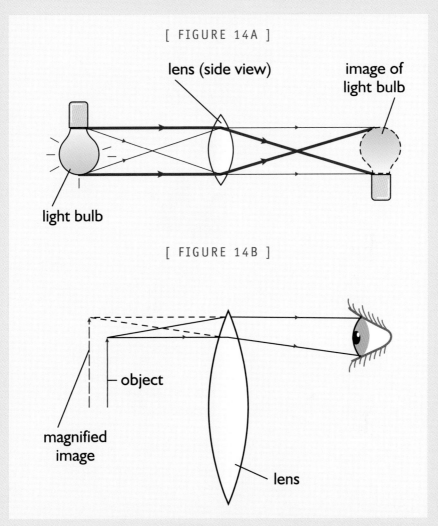

[FIGURE 14A]

lens (side view)

image of
light bulb

light bulb

[FIGURE 14B]

object

magnified
image

lens

a) To form an image on a white card, the lens must bend the light as shown. b) To form an upright, magnified image, the lens is held near the object. The drawing shows how the lens bends the light to form a magnified image. The dotted lines show where refracted light rays going to the eye appear to come from.

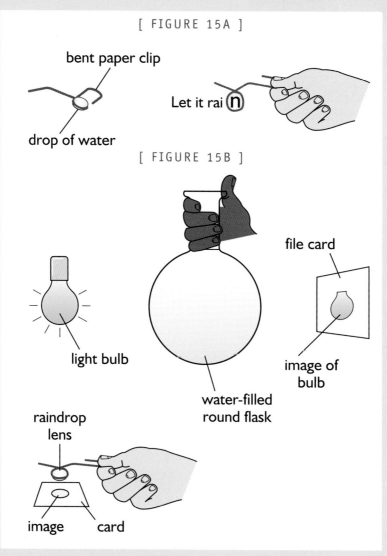

[FIGURE 15A]

bent paper clip

Let it rain

drop of water

[FIGURE 15B]

file card

light bulb

image of bulb

water-filled round flask

raindrop lens

image   card

a) A raindrop lens is made by placing a drop of water on a bent paper clip. The water drop can be used to magnify print. b) Use the same lens to "capture" an image of a lightbulb on a file card. You can make a larger raindrop lens by using a round water-filled flask or a brandy glass.

lens to magnify the print in this book. Place the lens on the print. Look through the lens and raise it toward your eye until you can see the image of the print clearly. Figure 14b shows how the lens bends light to form a magnified image. The light rays from the object that pass through the lens are bent so that they appear to come from an enlarged image.

Now repeat the experiment, this time with a water lens. Make a raindrop lens by using an eyedropper to place a drop of water on a bent paper clip, as shown in Figure 15. (As in the previous experiment, you may want to use the larger water lens by filling a Florence flask or brandy glass with water.) Hold the raindrop lens close to some fine print in a magazine resting in bright light. Even though you may be able to see only one letter or part of one letter through the lens, you will be able to tell that it is magnified. As you can see, the raindrop lens magnifies the print, just as a glass lens does.

NATURAL RAINBOWS

Now that you have seen how water can both reflect and refract light, you can understand how a rainbow is formed by raindrops. Some of the sunlight entering a raindrop near its top is bent, reflected off the back surface, and then refracted (bent) again as it emerges from the lower front of the drop. Because light of different colors is bent by different amounts, the colors are separated when the light is refracted as it enters and leaves a raindrop. In Figure 16a, only two rays of colored light—red (R) and violet (V)—are shown. These two colors, as you know, are at the edges of the multicolored rainbow. They mark the limits of our color vision. There are other colors, such as ultraviolet and infrared, but we cannot see them.

At point A, where the sunlight shown in Figure 16a is refracted, some light, not shown in the drawing, is reflected from the surface of the drop. At point X, where light is shown being reflected back into the drop, some light is refracted as it passes through the drop. The inside of

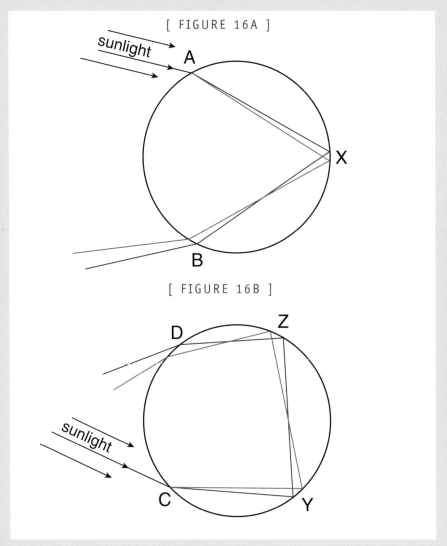

sunlight

A

X

B

D

Z

sunlight

C

Y

Sunlight is shown entering raindrops where it is refracted and reflected. The different colors in white light are refracted by different amounts, causing the colors to separate. a) Light is refracted at A and B and reflected at X. The light emerging from this drop forms part of the primary rainbow. b) Light is refracted at C and D and reflected twice (at Y and Z). Light emerging from this drop is part of the secondary rainbow.

the drop is not a perfect mirror; some light passes through water and is refracted. Again, at point B, where the light is shown being refracted as it reenters the air, some of the light striking point B is reflected back into the drop.

The fainter secondary rainbow is caused by sunlight that enters the lower front of a raindrop at C, as shown in Figure 16b. This light is also separated into different colors (shown here as R and V) when it is refracted upon entering the drop. The light that we see as the secondary rainbow is reflected twice inside the drops, at Y and Z, before it is refracted again as it emerges from the upper front portion of the rain-drop at D. Of course, at each point where the light is reflected, some light is also refracted as it reenters the air. And at points C and D, where light is refracted, some light (not shown) is reflected.

The diagrams in Figure 16 show how the violet and red rays of light are reflected and refracted to an observer's eyes by a raindrop. But, as you can see from the drawing, the red and violet light leave the drop at different angles. Only one of the rays (R or V, but not both) would reach

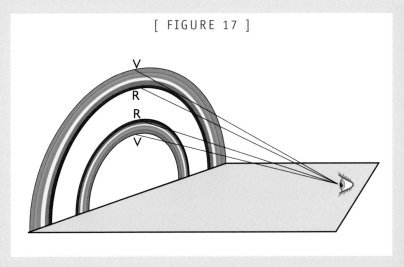

[FIGURE 17]

A rainbow is made from an arc of falling raindrops.

the observer's eyes. The red that we see in a rainbow must come from different drops than the violet and other colors that we see.

In Figure 17, you see that a rainbow is made by an arc of falling raindrops. The red light in a primary (brighter) rainbow comes to us from the drops along its outer edge. The violet light comes from drops along the arc's inner edge. The colors in between red and violet reach us from drops that lie between the edges of the rainbow. For the violet light, the angle between the observer and the light rays that we see coming to our eyes from the arc of falling raindrops is 40 degrees. For the red light, the angle is 42 degrees.

In the case of the secondary (dimmer) rainbow, the angle from the observer to the violet light is 54 degrees; for the red light, the angle is 50 degrees. For both rainbows, the spectrum of colors along the two arcs will continue to reach our eyes as long as the sun shines and falling raindrops continue to replace those that have fallen below the rainbows' arcs.

OTHER COLORS FROM RAIN IN THE SKY

Rainbows caused by moonlight reflected from falling raindrops also occur. With your back to a full moon on one side of the sky, you may see a faint rainbow if rain is falling from the opposite side of the sky. Such rainbows, called lunar bows, are dim and, generally, only the red to yellow portion of the bow is bright enough to be visible.

Halos are seen quite frequently. They are faint rainbow-like rings around the sun or moon. They are caused by light refracted from tiny ice crystals in high cirrus clouds. The ice acts like tiny prisms spreading the sunlight or moonlight into a spectrum. Often a double halo is seen; the brighter, inner one can be seen at an angle of 22 degrees and the outer one at 46 degrees. Because the crystals are turned at various angles, the colors are mixed, but usually the inner portion of the ring has a reddish tint.

Sometimes when the sun or moon shines through a thin fog, you may see a colored ring with the sun or moon at its center. This is caused by light diffracting (spreading out) around the fog droplets. This corona, as it is called, is easily distinguished from a halo. Unlike a halo, which is reddish around its inside, the red in a corona is around its outside.

"Sun dogs" or "mock suns" are fairly common in polar regions. They also are seen in other regions when the sun is close to the horizon because of time of day or time of year. They are part of the halos described earlier. They are much brighter than the rest of the halo and lie to either side of the sun. Their brightness is due to the fact that the ice crystals in the cirrus clouds that cause sun dogs reflect, as well as refract, a lot of sunlight.

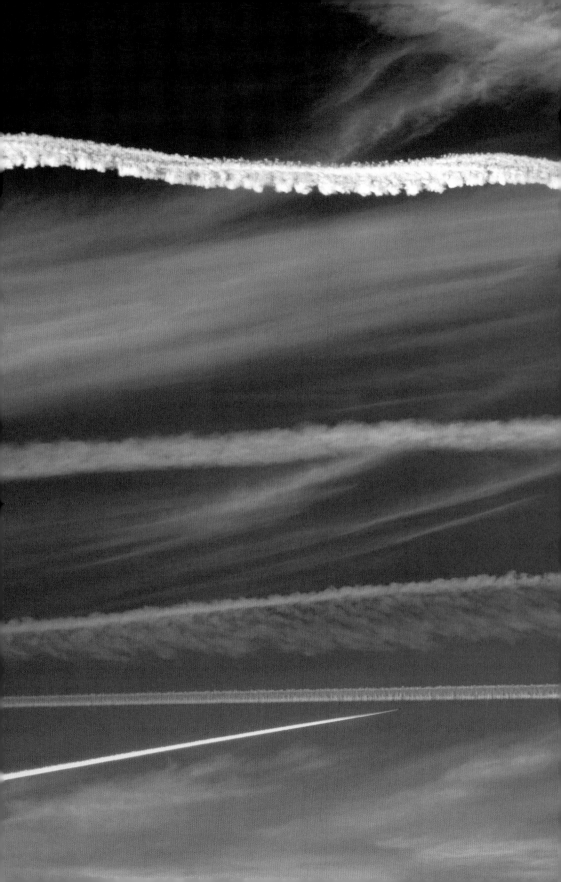

Chapter 5

Clouds: Droplets of Water in the Sky

WHEN WARM, MOIST AIR RISES, IT EXPANDS AND COOLS. The water vapor in the cool air begins to condense, forming tiny water droplets. Billions and trillions of these tiny droplets make up the clouds you see in the sky.

Clouds that form when the moisture in cool, expanding air condenses are natural clouds. They have probably existed for almost as long as Earth. But today we see other clouds, clouds that are the result of a human presence on Earth. One of the most common of these is the vapor trail left by jet airplanes. The water vapor coming from the engines' exhaust cools rapidly and condenses. The condensed droplets form the familiar jet trail "clouds" that mark the path of high-flying jet airplanes. In very dry air, these jet trails disappear very quickly. But in still, moist air they may persist for a long time. Of course, wind will break up the trails quickly.

CLOUDS AND MORE CLOUDS

You have probably lived long enough to know that some clouds indicate rain, while others are commonly found on fair-weather days. Fluffy, white, cauliflower-like, distinctly-shaped clouds that resemble heaps of loose cotton are fair weather clouds. They are called cumulus clouds, one of the three basic types of clouds. The other two are stratus and cirrus clouds. Stratus clouds usually cover the sky like gray blankets. At ground level, stratus clouds are called fog. Cirrus clouds are high, thin, wispy, feathery clouds. Sometimes they are called mare's tails because they resemble the long, thin hair found in a horse's tail.

Figures 18a–18c contain photographs of these three basic cloud types. Meteorologists break these three basic types of clouds into more subtle classifications. If you would like to learn to identify the many cloud types, you can buy a small guide book for clouds or study a book on meteorology.

Examples of the three basic types of clouds: a) cirrus; b) cumulus; c) stratus.

Materials:

- an adult
- mirror
- heavy piece of cardboard approximately 25 cm x 50 cm (10 in x 20 in)
- water
- stove
- kettle
- ice cubes
- small bowl or pie pan
- salt
- coffee mug
- flexible drinking straw

On a cold day, you may have "seen your breath." What you saw was water vapor, a normal part of the air you exhale, condensing into tiny droplets as it came in contact with the cold air. On other cold days, you may have looked in vain trying to "see your breath." Can you explain why you can see your breath on some cold days but not on others? In this experiment, you will begin by using your breath to form the particles that make up a cloud, even in the absence of cold air.

To see how the droplets in a cloud form, hold your open mouth close to a mirror and blow gently. The mirror becomes coated with a fine layer of tiny water droplets. In the same way, moisture condenses from air. As the air cools, water condenses, forming the tiny droplets that make up a cloud.

To make a three-dimensional cloud, fold a heavy piece of cardboard about 25 cm (10 in) high by 50 cm (20 in) long, as shown in Figure 19. **Ask an adult** to boil some water while you place a few ice cubes in a small bowl or pie pan. Add some salt to the ice to make it even colder. Place the bowl or pan on the folded cardboard as shown. **Ask the adult** to place a mug half-filled with the hot water underneath the cold bowl. Can you see a cloud form where the hot, moist air touches the cold bowl?

To make the cloud bigger, **ask the adult** to use a flexible drinking straw to gently blow bubbles in the hot water. What effect does this have on the cloud that forms near the cold bowl?

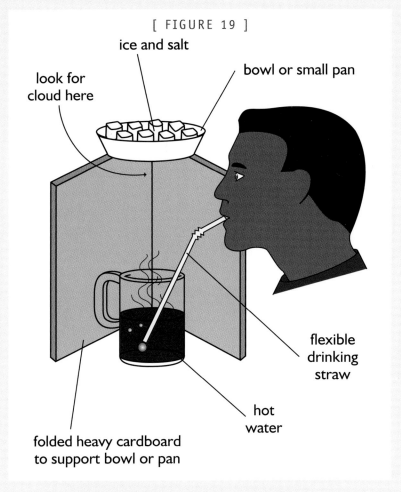

[FIGURE 19]

ice and salt

look for cloud here

bowl or small pan

flexible drinking straw

folded heavy cardboard to support bowl or pan

hot water

You can make a cloud in your kitchen.

Materials:

- an adult
- 1-L or 2-L clear plastic soda bottle with screw-on cap
- cup
- water
- a friend
- flashlight or small lamp
- matches
- dark room

Remove the paper labels from a clear 1-L or 2-L plastic soda bottle. Pour about half a cup of water into the bottle, screw the cap back on, and shake the bottle vigorously for about 30 seconds. This should saturate the air in the bottle with moisture. Pour out all but about a tablespoon of water, and screw the cap back onto the bottle. Darken the room and ask a friend to shine a flashlight or a small lamp through the bottle while you squeeze the bottle with both hands (see Figure 20). By squeezing the bottle, you increase the pressure on the moist air inside. Now, release the bottle so that the pressure quickly decreases. Do you see any evidence of a cloud forming in the bottle?

Repeat the experiment, but before you screw the cap on for the second time, **ask an adult** to light a match, blow it out, and hold it inside the bottle so that smoke particles enter the bottle. If you have trouble getting smoke into the bottle, try squeezing the sides of the bottle before the match is lit. After the match is blown out and held near the mouth of the bottle, release the sides of the bottle. Air will enter the expanding bottle, dragging the smoke along with it.

Once you have gotten smoke into the bottle, screw the cap on securely. Shake the bottle again to be sure the air is saturated with moisture. Have your friend shine the light through the bottle while you squeeze the bottle and then quickly release it. Do you see any evidence of a cloud forming in the bottle this time?

CLOUDS

As you have seen in the previous two experiments, clouds form when moist air cools or when air pressure decreases. However, there have to be small particles (nuclei) on which the water droplets can condense. In your experiment, those particles came from the smoke. Actually, when air pressure decreases, the expanding air cools. You have probably seen the opposite effect; when air pressure increases, the temperature of that air increases. That is why your bicycle pump becomes hot when you pump air into a tire. When you push the pump's piston into the cylinder and squeeze the air together, forcing it into the tire, the air gets hotter. Some of that heat flows into the pump and you can feel its added warmth.

[FIGURE 20]

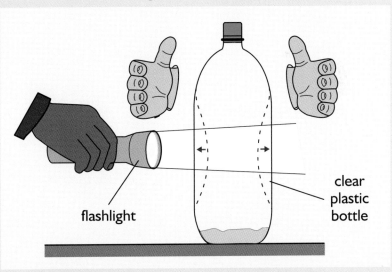

flashlight

clear plastic bottle

Does a cloud form when air pressure decreases, or is something else needed?

In the atmosphere, there are usually lots of tiny particles that can serve as nuclei for condensation. Particles of smoke, pollen, and tiny salt crystals from the oceans are usually present. As warm, moist air rises into the atmosphere, the pressure at higher altitudes is usually less and so the air cools. The moisture in the cool, low-pressure air begins to condense on tiny nuclei. On a warm summer afternoon, you can see puffy, white cumulus clouds form. The moisture in the rising air cools and condenses, forming the tiny droplets that make up a cloud. Experiment 5.3 will show you why the warm air rises.

5.3 Warm Fluids in Cold Fluids

Materials:

- outdoor thermometer
- small box
- closed room
- pen or pencil
- notebook
- watch or clock
- tape
- cold water
- 2 small transparent glasses or vials
- warm water
- food coloring
- eyedropper

Place a thermometer on the floor near the center of a closed room. To make sure no one steps on it, put the thermometer in a small open box. After about five minutes, record the temperature.

Next, place the thermometer near the ceiling. If there is no way to support the thermometer, ask permission to tape it to something near the ceiling. After about five minutes, read the thermometer. How does the temperature near the ceiling compare with the temperature near the floor? What does this tell you about warm air as compared with cold air?

A fluid is any material that takes the shape of the container in which it is placed. Both air (a gas) and water (a liquid) are fluids. Does warm water rise in cold water the way warm air rises above cold air?

To find out, place some cold water in a small transparent glass or vial. Put some warm water into another glass or vial. Color the warm water with a drop or two of food coloring. Stir the colored warm water. Use an eyedropper to remove some of the warm water. Place the end of the eyedropper down into the cold water and very gently squeeze the warm colored water into the clear cold water, as shown in Figure 21. Does the warm water rise or sink in the cold water? Does warm water in cold water behave like warm air in cold air?

HUMIDITY AND DEW POINT

Moisture will condense from the air only if the temperature is at or below the dew point. The dew point is the temperature at which the air becomes saturated with moisture. Saturated means that the air holds as

[FIGURE 21]

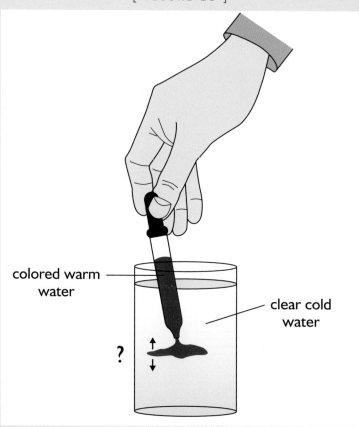

colored warm water

clear cold water

?

Will warm water rise or sink in cold water?

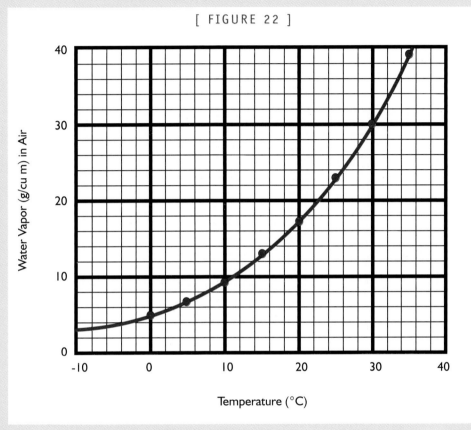

[FIGURE 22]

The graph shows the maximum amount of water vapor that can be found in one cubic meter of air at different temperatures.

much moisture as it possibly can. Table 1 in Chapter 2 shows the greatest amount of water vapor that can be found in a cubic meter (cu m) of air at different temperatures.

How can you use the graph in Figure 22 to determine the water vapor per cubic meter of air for temperatures that lie between, above, or below those in Table 1? As you can see from the table and graph, warm air can hold more water vapor than cold air. The amount of moisture that a cubic meter of air can hold at a particular temperature is called the absolute humidity. Air at 30°C (86°F) can hold 30.0 g of water vapor before it is saturated. The absolute humidity of air at 30°C is, therefore, 30.0 g/cu m. If air at that temperature actually holds 15.0 g, we say the relative humidity of the air is 50 percent because it holds half the moisture it could hold. What is the relative humidity of air at 30°C if it actually contains 7.5 g of water vapor per cubic meter?

How do we know how much water vapor the air actually contains? There are various ways that chemists can separate water vapor from the other gases in air saturated with water. By doing so, the amount of water that was dissolved in the air can be weighed. That is how the information in Table 1 was originally obtained. But once that table was available, it became much easier to determine the absolute and relative humidity of air. This is done by finding the dew point.

Materials:

- warm water
- shiny metal can
- outdoor thermometer
- pen or pencil
- notebook
- small pieces of ice

You can determine the absolute and relative humidity of the air by finding the dew point. The dew point is the temperature at which moisture begins to condense from the air. You have probably noticed that you often find moisture on the outside of a glass that contains cold milk or soda. The moisture comes from water vapor in the warm air that condenses when the air comes in contact with the cold glass.

Suppose that you have a glass that contains water at 20°C (68°F). If you cool the water by adding ice, you may find that moisture (dew) begins to collect on the glass when the temperature of the water reaches 10°C (50°F). Since water is condensing on the glass, it must mean the air in contact with the glass became saturated when the temperature reached 10°C. From Table 1, we know that at 10°C the absolute humidity of the air is 9.3 g/cu m. At 20°C, the air could hold as much as 17.1 g. Therefore, the air holds only a fraction of the moisture it could hold at 20°C. That fraction is 9.3 ÷ 17.1. The relative humidity then is 9.3 ÷ 17.1 = 0.54 = 54%.

To determine the dew point of the air in a room or outdoors on a warm day, pour some warm water into a shiny metal can. Place a thermometer in the water and stir the liquid. When the liquid in the thermometer stops moving, record the temperature of the water in your science notebook. Then add a small piece of ice to the water and continue to stir as you watch the side of the shiny can. Continue to stir and add small pieces of ice to the water until you see tiny droplets of moisture condensing on the can. At the moment you see the droplets, read the thermometer and record the temperature. That temperature is the dew point. Use the dew point to find the relative humidity.

Repeat this experiment on different days and at different times of the year. How is the dew point affected by the weather? During which season of the year is the dew point temperature lowest in your home or school? During which season is the dew point temperature highest?

 Science Fair Project Idea

Suppose someone believes that the moisture on the shiny can is caused by water leaking through the cold can and not by water in the air condensing on the outside of the can. Design one or more experiments to show that the water does not leak through the can.

Chapter 6

Snow: Tiny Crystals of Ice

WHEN THE AIR IS VERY COLD, THE WATER DROPLETS THAT MAKE UP CLOUDS MAY FREEZE, FORMING TINY CRYSTALS OF ICE. These crystals collide with one another to form snowflakes. As the snowflakes grow, they begin to fall. If the air below the clouds is above freezing, the snowflakes melt and reach the ground as cold rain. But if the air is below the freezing point, the flakes will retain their crystalline structure and fall as snow.

But snow, like rain, does not fall evenly on Earth's surface. Some places, where freezing temperatures are rare, such as Miami, Florida, never see snow. The average annual snowfall in Syracuse, New York is 293.6 cm (115.6 in). Portland, Oregon, despite being located at approximately the same latitude, receives an average annual snowfall of 16.5 cm (6.5 in). Clearly, snow does not fall evenly in terms of space or time.

If a snowstorm is accompanied by winds of 56 kph (35 mph) or more and visibility is reduced to less than 4/10 km (1/4 mi) for at least three hours, the storm is defined as a blizzard. One of the worst blizzards in history occurred during the four-day period of March 11–14, 1888. The famous blizzard of '88 blanketed the northeastern United States, caused 400 deaths, and left New York City buried in 6-m (20-ft) drifts. In January, 1952, a blizzard that piled up 15-m (50-ft) drifts near the Donner Pass in California's mountains left the *City of San Francisco* passenger train stalled in snow. Three days passed before rescue crews could reach the 226 passengers and crew.

Materials:

- ruler or meterstick or yardstick
- sticks
- snow
- shovel
- large container with straight sides used in Experiment 3.1
- narrow transparent container with straight sides used in Experiment 3.1.

Unless the wind blows as the snow falls, it is easy to measure a snowfall. All you have to do is go to an open area and stick a ruler or meterstick straight down into the snow until it reaches the ground. The level of the snow on the ruler indicates the number of millimeters or inches of snowfall. If you mark this area with sticks, you can shovel away the snow and return to the same place to measure the next snowfall.

If the wind blows the snow into drifts, it is more difficult to measure snowfall accurately. You will have to measure the depth of the snow in a number of different places and find the average depth. You can do this by adding all the depths you measure and then dividing the sum by the number of measurements.

Total precipitation is measured as millimeters (or inches) of rain. To convert the depth of new-fallen snow into millimeters (or inches) of rain, fill the tall can or container you used to collect rain in Experiment 3.1 with the loose snow. Be careful not to pack the snow into the container. Bring the can inside and let the snow melt. As soon as all the snow has melted, pour the liquid into the narrower container you used to measure rainfall in Experiment 3.1. How many millimeters (or inches) of precipitation fell?

From the depth of the can and the depth of the water that forms when the snow melts, you can find how many millimeters (or inches) of rain would have fallen if the water had not frozen in the clouds. For example, if the snow in the can was 250 mm (10 in) deep and you found that the melted snow was equal to 12.5 mm (0.5 in) of rain, then you know that 250 mm (10 in) of the snowfall is equal to 12.5 mm (0.5 in) of rain. What depth of this snowfall would be required to produce 25 mm (1 in) of rain?

Collect samples of snow from different storms throughout the winter. Is the amount of snow needed to produce 25 mm (1 in) of rain always the same or does it vary with the type of snow? Does a foot of loose, dry, fluffy snow contain as much precipitation as a foot of heavy, wet snow?

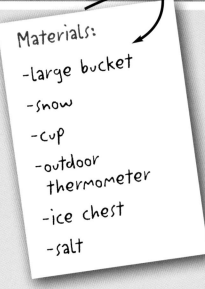

Materials:

- large bucket
- snow
- cup
- outdoor thermometer
- ice chest
- salt

Take a large bucket outside. Fill it with snow and bring it indoors. Scoop out a cupful of the snow. Place a thermometer in the cup and see what happens to the temperature. Stir the snow with the thermometer until the temperature stops falling. Does the temperature of the melting snow remain constant? What is the temperature of the melting snow?

What do you think is the temperature of the melting snow in the bucket? Place the thermometer in the big bucket of snow and stir the snow with the thermometer. Then read the thermometer. What is the temperature of the melting snow in the bucket?

Fill a large ice chest with snow and bring it inside. What do you think is the temperature of the snow melting in the ice chest? Use a thermometer to measure the temperature of the melting snow. Was it the temperature you predicted? Does the temperature of melting snow depend on the amount of snow that is melting?

Pour some salt into a cup of melting snow. What happens to the temperature of melting snow when you add salt? Why do you think people throw salt on icy walks and roads?

6.3 Examining Snowflakes

Materials:
- magnifying glass
- warm jacket

You may have heard that snowflakes are hexagonal (six-sided) and that no two snowflakes are alike. You can look at snowflakes quite easily. Next time it snows, go outside with a magnifying glass in your jacket pocket. Allow some time for the outside of your clothing to become cold. Then let a few snowflakes fall on the sleeve of your jacket. Use the magnifier to look at the flakes. Because the warm air from your lungs will melt the snowflakes, you will have to hold your breath as you examine them.

[FIGURE 23]

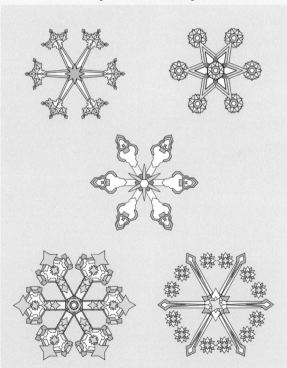

These are examples of some typically beautiful snowflakes.

Do the snowflakes look like the ones in Figure 23? Are they all hexagonal? Are any two the same?

When snowflakes first form, they are hexagons. However, as they fall they may bump into one another and break or stick together. If the air is warm, the crystals may melt or partially melt. As a result, snowflakes are often not the same when they land as they were when they first formed in a cloud.

 Science Fair Project Idea

Examine snowflakes from different storms and at different times during the same storm. Do the flakes from some storms have different characteristic shapes than those from another storm? Do flakes from the same storm change appearance as the storm progresses?

6.4 Melting Snow Faster

Materials:

-10-cm x 10-cm (4-in x 4-in) squares of white, black, and various colored construction paper

- snow

- sunlight

On a calm, clear day, place 10-cm x 10-cm (4-in x 4-in) squares of white, black, and various colored construction paper on top of some snow in sunlight. After a few hours, look at the squares. Under which square has more snow melted? How does this experiment help you to understand why you should wear dark clothing outside in the winter and white clothing in the summer?

One South American country spread black carbon dust over its mountain glaciers during the summer in an effort to increase its water supply. Why do you think they expected such a process would help to solve their water shortage?

6.5 Preventing Snow From Melting

Materials:

- snow or ice cubes
- several friends
- insulated (Styrofoam) cups
- newspapers
- small boxes
- paper towels
- aluminum foil
- other insulating materials

Many homes are insulated. This means the walls, ceilings, and floors are covered with materials that reduce the rate at which heat can escape in the winter and enter in the summer. Perhaps you can find ways to insulate a cup of snow and increase the time required for it to melt. You might ask your friends to enter a contest in which everyone is given a cupful of snow or an ice cube. The object of the contest is to see who can keep the snow or ice from completely melting for the longest time.

Of course, you will have to agree on some rules, such as forbidding the placing of snow in refrigerators, freezers, and other cold places. You might want to supply some materials such as insulated (Styrofoam) cups, newspapers, small boxes, paper towels, aluminum foil, and other items that contestants may suggest.

Who can keep the snow or ice cube for the longest period? What methods were used to reduce melting? After contestants have a chance to discuss their various methods for keeping snow or ice from melting, you might hold a second contest. Are the contestants more successful in this second competition? Does the same person win for a second time or does a new winner emerge?

FURTHER READING

BOOKS

Bochinski, Julianne Blair. *The Complete Workbook for Science Fair Projects.* Hoboken, N.J.: John Wiley and Sons, Inc., 2004.

Carson, Mary Kay. *Weather Projects for Young Scientists: Experiments and Science Fair Ideas.* Chicago: Chicago Review Press, 2007.

Henson, Robert. *The Rough Guide to Weather.* New York: Penguin Putnam, Inc., 2007.

Howell, Laura. *The Usborne Internet-Linked Introduction to Weather & Climate Change.* London, UK: Usborne Publishing Ltd., 2003.

Moorman, Thomas. *How to Make Your Science Project Scientific.* Revised Edition. New York: John Wiley & Sons, Inc., 2002.

INTERNET ADDRESSES

Society for Science and the Public. *Science News for Kids.* 2000–2008.
http://www.sciencenews.org

United States General Services Administration. *Kids.Gov.* 2008.
http://www.kids.gov

Wicker, Crystal. *Weather Wiz Kids.* 2003–2008.
http://www.weatherwizkids.com

INDEX

INDEX

INDEX